SIR GAWAIN AND THE GREEN KNIGHT

RENDERED LITERALLY INTO MODERN ENGLISH
PROM THE ALLITERATIVE ROMANCE-POEM OF
A.D. 1360, FROM COTTON MS NERO A X
IN BRITISH MUSEUM

BY
REV. ERNEST J. B. KIRTLAN
B.A. (LONDON), B.D. (ST. ANDREWS)

DECORATED BY
FREDERIC LAWRENCE

LONDON
CHARLES H. KELLY
25–35 CITY ROAD, AND 26 PATERNOSTER ROW, E.C.

1912

THIS EDITION was adapted from various print and digital versions in the public domain, based on the Reverend Ernest J.B. Kirtlan's translation, and including Frederic Lawrence's illustrations and decorations (London: Kelly, 1912).

Sir Gawain & the Green Knight
From the Pearl Manuscript, ca. AD 1380
The British Library
MS Cotton Nero A.x/2, ff94^v–130^r

ISBN: 978-1-947587-18-2
Fox Editing Classics
First paperback edition

Copyright 2023 Katie Fox
Fox Editing & Publishing
San Francisco, CA

FOXEDITING.COM

CONTENTS

Canto the First	1
Canto the Second	25
Canto the Third	61
Canto the Fourth	107

'Sir Gawain hath sought the isles of Light
    Beyond the shores of day,
Where moon never waneth to shades of night
    And the silver fountains play.
There he holdeth high court as the maiden's knight
    In the maiden's isle for ay.'

Sir Gawain and The Green Knight
Canto the first

AFTER the siege and the assault of Troy, when the city was burned to ashes, the knight who therein wrought treason was tried for his treachery and was found to be the truest on earth. Aeneas the noble it was, and his high kindred, who vanquished great nations and became the rulers of wellnigh all the western world. Noble Romulus went to Rome with great show of strength, and

built that city at the first, and gave it his own name, as it is called to this day. Ticius went into Tuscany and began to set up habitations, and Langobard made his home in Lombardy; whilst Brutus, far over the French sea by many a full broad hillside, the fair land of Britain
did win,
Where war and wrack and wonder
Often were seen therein,
And oft both bliss and blunder
Have come about through sin.

II

NOW, when Britain was conquered by this noble man, brave warriors were bred and born therein that were fond of striving, so that many times sorrow came thereof. And more wonders have been wrought in this land than in any other I wot of since that time. But of all the British kings, Arthur was the most courteous, as I have heard say. And I propose to tell you a wondrous adventure, as some hold it to

be, that happened in Arthur's court; and if ye will listen but a little I will tell it you
>with tongue

>>As I have heard it told,
>In a story brave and strong,
>>In a loyal book of old,
>In the land it has been long.

III

THIS King Arthur was at Camelot at Christmas with many a lovely lord, and they were all princely brethren of the Round Table, and they made rich revel and mirth, and were free from care. And betimes these gentle knights held full many a tournament, and jousted in jolly fashion, and then returned they to the court to sing the Christmas carols. And the feasting was for fifteen days, and it was with all the meat and mirth that men could devise. And glorious to hear was the noisy glee by day and the dancing by night, and all was joyous in hall and chamber, among the lords and ladies as it pleased them, and they were the most renowned knights

under Christ
and the loveliest ladies that ever lived; for all these fair folk were in their first age, and great were they

        in mirth
The gayest in the land,
The king was of great worth,
    I could not name a band
So hardy upon earth.

IV

AND when the New Year was come, on that day the nobles on the dais were double served, when the king came with his knights into the great hall and the chanting in the chapel was ended. And clerks and others set up a loud cry, and they kept the Feast of Christmas anew, and they gave and received New Year's gifts, and much talking was there about the gifts. And ladies laughed full loudly, though they had lost in the exchange, and he that won was not wroth, as ye will well trow, and they made all this mirth together as was fitting for the season.

When they had washed, they worthily went to their seats, each according to his rank, as was seemly. And Queen Guinevere was full gaily attired as she took her seat on the dais, and on fair silks under a canopy of costly Tarsian tapestry, embroidered with the finest of gems that money could buy on
>   a day
> The comeliest lady, I ween,
> She glanced from eyes that were grey,
>   Her like that he had seen
> Truly could no man say.

V

UT Arthur would not eat until all were served, for he was so jolly, and almost like a child. Little recked he of his life; and so restless was he that he could not sit or recline for long, so active was his young blood and his brain. And there was another strange thing about him because of his noble birth, that he would not eat on these high days until he had heard some eerie tale of marvellous adventures, of his forbears or arms, or else that some knight joined with another in

jousting, life for life as hap would have it. This was the custom of the King when he was in court at each feast as it came amongst his noble household
>   in hall,
> Therefore so bold of face
> He sat there, strong in stall,
>   In that new year of grace
> Much mirth he made with all.

VI

THUS was the King in the high seat talking before the high table of courteous trifles and good. Sir Gawain was sitting beside Guinevere. Agravayn of the hard hand sat on the other side, and both were sons of the king's sister and very strong and faithful knights. Bishop Bawdewyn was at the head of the table, and Ywain, son of Urien, was eating by himself. And they were all on the dais, and well were they served, and afterwards many a true man at the sideboards. With the crashing of trumpets came the first course, and with banners and beating of drums and piping loud, so that many a heart

heaved full high at the sound, and there were many dear and full dainty meats. And there were so many dishes and such great plenty that it was hard to find room to set before the folk the silver service that held the courses
>on cloth,
>Each man as he loved himself
>There laughed he without loath,
>Each two had dishes twelve,
>Good beer and bright wine both.

VII

NOW will I tell you no more of the serving, for ye may wot well no want was there. Another and a full new wonder was drawing near. Scarcely had the noise ceased and the first course been served in the court, when there came in at the hall door an ugly fellow and tallest of all men upon earth. From his neck to his loins so square set was he, and so long and stalwart of limb, that I trow he was half a giant. And yet he was a man, and the merriest that might ride. His body in back and breast was strong, his belly and waist were very

small, and all his features
> full clean.
> Great wonder of the knight
Folk had in hall, I ween,
> Full fierce he was to sight,
And over all bright green.

VIII

ND he was all clad in green garments, and fitting close to his sides was a straight coat with a simple mantle above it and well lined with gay and bright furs, as was also his hood hanging about his locks and round his shoulders; and he had hosen of that same green on his calves, and bright spurs of gold, that hung down his legs upon silk borders, richly striped, where his foot rested in the stirrup.

And verily all his vesture was of pure green, both the stripings of his belt, and the stones that shone brightly in his gorgeous apparel, upon silk work, on his person and saddle; and it would be too tedious to tell you even the half of such trifles as were thereon embroidered with birds and flies in gaudy greens, and ever gold in the midst. The pendants of the hores's neck-gear, the proud crupper, the ornaments, and all the metal thereof, were enamelled of green; the stirrups that he stood in of the same colour, and his saddle-bow also; and they were all glimmering and shining with green stones; and the foal on which he rode was of that same hue

>certain
>A green horse great and thick,
>A steed full strong to strain,
>In broidered bridle thick,
>To the man he was full gain.

IX

THUS gaily was this man dressed out in green, and the hair of the horse's head was of green, and his fair, flowing locks clung about his shoulders; and a great beard like a bush hung over his breast, and with his noble hair was cut evenly all round above his elbows, and the lower part of his sleeves was fastened like a king's mantle. The horse's mane was crisped and gemmed with many a knot, and folded in with gold thread about the fair green with ever a fillet of hair and one of gold, and his tail and head were intertwisted with gold in the same manner, and bound with a band of bright green, and decked with costly stones and tied with a tight knot above; and about them were ringing many full bright bells of burnished gold. Such a horse or his rider were never seen in that hall before or with eye.

'He looks like flashing light,'
Say they that him descry,
'It seemed that no man might
His dintings e'er defy.'

X

AND he had no helmet nor hauberk, nor was he armour-plated, nor had he spear or shield with which to smite; but in one hand he held a holly branch, that is most green when the groves are all bare, and in the other he held an axe, huge and uncanny, and a sharp weapon was it to describe whoso might wish. And the head thereof measured an ell, and its grain was of green steel and of hewn gold, and the broad edge of it was burnished brightly, and as well shaped for cutting

as a razor. And the sturdy knight gripped the steel of the stiff staff that was wound round with iron right along its length, and engraven in green with many noble deeds; and lace lapped it about and was fastened on the head, and looped about the handle full oft with many tassels tied thereto and broidered full richly on buttons of bright green. And the man haled into the hall, and pushed forward to the high dais, fearful of nothing, and saluted no one, but looked scornfully over them all. The first word that he uttered was 'Where is the chief of this company? Gladly would I see that man in the body, and speak with him seasonably
in town.'

  The knight cast round his eye,
And reeled up and down,
  He stopped and 'gan to spy
Who was of best renown.

XI

HEN they all looked at him, and every man marvelled much what it might mean that a man and his horse should be of such a colour of green, green as the grass and greener, as it seemed, than green enamel

upon gold shining brightly. All studied him carefully, and came nearer to him, for they had seen many wonders, but nothing like unto this; therefore the folk deemed it to be a phantom or some faery. And many of them were afraid to answer him; astounded at his voice, stone still they sat. And there was a solemn silence through that rich hall, as though they had all fallen asleep
speedily;
Not all, I trow, for fear
But some for courtesy:
Let him whom all hold dear
Unto him make reply.

XII

HEN Arthur on the high dais beheld that adventure, and royally did reverence unto him, for nothing could affright him, and he said, 'Sir, welcome art thou to this hall. I am Arthur, the head of this hostel. Alight from thy horse, and linger with us, I pray thee, and afterwards we will come to know what thy will is.' 'Nay,' quoth that fellow, 'As He that sitteth on high shall help me, it is not mine errand to dwell any while in this place, but I am come because the fame of thy knights is so highly praised, and thy burgesses and thy town are held to be the best in the world, and the strongest riders on horses in steel armour, and the bravest and the worthiest of all mankind, and proof in playing in all joustings; and here, too, courtesy is well known, as I have heard say; and it is for these reasons that I am come hither at this time. Thou mayest rest assured by this holly token I hold in my hand that I am come in peaceful wise, and seek no quarrel; for had I come in company, in fighting wise, I have both a helm and a hauberk at home, and a shield, and a sharp and brightly shining spear, and other weapons I wield there as I ween; but because I wage no warfare, my weeds are of softer sort. But if thou art so bold as all men say, thou wilt grant me in goodly wise the games I ask by right.'

  Then Arthur he did swear,
And said, 'Sir courteous knight,
  If thou cravest battle bare
Thou shalt not fail to fight.'

XIII

'NAY, I tell thee in good faith, I seek not to fight, for the men on this bench are but beardless children, and if I were hasped in arms on a high steed there is no man here to match with me. I only crave of this court a Christmas game, as this is the feast of Yule and New Year, and many here are brave. And if any in this house holds himself so hardy and is so bold-blooded and so utterly mad that he dare strike one stroke for another in return, I will give to him this costly axe, that is heavy enough, and he shall handle it if he likes, and I will bide the first blow as bare as I sit here. If any fellow here be so brave as to do what I say, let him come forward quickly and take hold of the weapon, and I will quit claim upon it for ever. It shall be his very own. And I will stand strongly on this floor to abide his stroke if thou wilt doom him to receive another stroke in return from me; yet will I grant him

          delay.

    I'll give to him the blow,
In a twelvemonth and a day.
    Now think and let me know
Dare any herein aught say.'

XIV

NOW, if this man astonished them at the first, even still more were they astonished at this word, both high and low. The man rode firm in the saddle, and rolled his red eyes about, and bent his rough, green shining eyebrows, and stroked his beard, waiting for some one to rise. And when no one would answer him, he coughed loudly and scornfully, and said, 'What! is this Arthur's house that all men are talking of? Where are now your pride and your valour, your wrath and fury and great words? for now is the revel and renown of the Round Table overcome by one word, for all of you are terrified though no blow has been struck.' Then he laughed so loudly that King Arthur was grieved thereat, and the blood, for shame, shot upwards into his bright face
>   so dear.

> He waxed as wroth as wind,
> So did all that were there,

The king was bravely kind,
And stood that strong man near.

XV

ND he said, 'By heaven, fellow, thy asking is strange, and since thou dost seek after foolishness, it behoves thee to find it. I know of no single man among us that is aghast at thy great words. Give me thy axe, for God's sake, and I will grant thee the boon thou cravest.' Arthur leapt forward towards him and caught him by the hand. Then fiercely alighted that other fellow from his horse. Arthur seized the axe, gripping it by the handle, and strongly brandished it about. The strong man stood towering before him, higher than any in the house, by his head and more. Stern of mien, he stood there and stroked his beard, and with face unmoved he drew down his coat, no more dismayed for the dints he was to receive than if any man upon the bench had brought him to drink
of wine.
Gawain sat by the queen,

To the king he did incline,
  *I tell thee truth I ween,
This mêlée must be mine.'

XVI

'F thou wilt allow me to come down from this bench and without fault leave this table and stand by thee there, and if my liege lady likes it not ill, I will come to thine aid before all this noble court; for methinks it not seemly that when such a thing as this is asked in this great hall, that thou shouldest deal with it thyself, though thou be eager to do so, when there are so many brave men about thee, on the benches, that, as I hope, under heaven, are not more precious than thou art, nor are they more able-bodied on the field, when there is any fighting. I am the weakest and most feeble of wit; and who seeketh truth knows that the loss of my life would be a small matter. I have no praise except that thou art mine uncle, and no goodness in my body have I except thy blood that flows in my veins. Since this affair is none of thine and I

have first made demand for it, it falls to me; and if I acquit not myself comely, let all this noble court
        me blame.'
    The knights whispered that day,
And all agreed the same
    The king must yield the fray,
And give Gawain the game.

XVII

HEN the king commanded the knight to rise up, which he readily did, and set himself fairly and knelt down again before the king and received from him the weapon, and the king lifted up his hand and gave him God's blessing, and prayed that both his heart and hand might be hardy and strong. 'Take care, cousin, that thou set one blow upon him, and if thou doest it well, then shalt thou bide the blow that he shall give thee afterwards.' Gawain went forward to the man with the axe in his hand, and the Green Knight boldly bided his coming and flinched not at all. Then said the Green Knight to

Sir Gawain, 'Let us make well our covenant ere we go further. First, I want to know thy name tell me truly.' 'In good faith,' said the knight, 'my name is Gawain, and it is Gawain that offers to give thee this blow, whatsoever befall him afterwards; and in a twelvemonth and a day thou shalt take back the blow with any weapon thou likest, if I shall be
>   alive.'
> That other answered again,
'Gawain, so may I thrive,
>   For I am fiercely fain
> Of the blow that thou wilt drive.'

XVIII

THEN said the Green Knight, 'Well it pleases me that I shall take at thy hand that which I sought in this hall. And thou hast truly rehearsed all the covenant I asked of the king; save that thou shalt pledge me to seek me thyself wheresoever thou dost hope to find me on the earth, and to fetch thee such wages as thou wilt deal me today in the presence of this noble company.' 'Oh tell me,' quoth Gawain, 'where must I seek thee? Where is thy place? By Him that made me, I wot not where thou dwellest, nor do I know thee, Sir Knight, nor thy court, nor thy name. But tell me that truly, and what is thy name, and I will use all my wit that I may win thither, and that I swear by my sooth.' 'It will suffice in the new year,' quoth the Green Knight to Gawain the gentle, 'if I tell thee truly when I have received the blow at thy hand. Then it is that I will quickly tell thee of my house, my home, and my name. Then mayest thou ask my faring, and hold the covenant, and if I say nothing at all, then will it speed thee better, for thou mayest linger in thy land and seek to fare no farther in search of such

    a sight.
 Take now the weapon grim,
Let us see how thou canst smite.'
 'Gladly,' said he to him;
Then stroked the axe that knight.

XIX

THE Green Knight then prepared himself, bowed down a little, and discovered his face, and his long and lovely locks fell flowing about his head and he bared the business in hand. Gawain gripped the axe and held it up aloft. He put his left foot forward, then he let the axe fall lightly down on the naked neck so that it sundered the bones, pierced through the flesh, so that the point of the steel bit into the ground, and the head of the Green Knight fell to the earth. And many kicked it with their feet as it rolled there, and blood rushed forth from the body and shone red on the green garments. Yet not a whit did the Green Knight falter nor fall, but started strongly forward on stiff shanks where the men were standing, and caught hold of his head and lifted it up. Then he went to his horse, seized the bridle, stepped into the saddle, and striding aloft, he held his head by the hair, and as gravely he sat in the saddle as

though no evil had befallen him and he were not headless
>in that stead.
He swayed his trunk about,
The ugly body that bled;
>Many of him had doubt
By the time his reasons were said.

XX

E held up the head in his hands, and addressed him to the dearest of those on the bench, to wit, Sir Gawain; and the eyelids were lifted up and looked forth, and the lips moved and said, 'Take heed, Sir Gawain, that thou art ready to go and seek me till thou find me as thou hast promised in this hall with these knights as witnesses. To the green chapel thou shalt come to receive such a blow as thou hast given, on New Year's morning. And many know me as the Knight of the Green Chapel. Fail not, then, to seek me until thou findest me; therefore come thou, or recreant shalt thou be called.' Then roughly he turned his reins, haled out of the hall door, with his head in his hand, and the horse's hoofs struck fire from the flinty stones. No one there knew of what kith or kin he was, or whence he came.

>Straightway
>Of the Green Knight they made light,
>Yet it was thought that day,
>A marvel, a wondrous sight,
>Though, laughing, they were gay.

XXI

OW, though Arthur the Gentle at this had great wonder, he let no semblance thereof be seen, but spake with gentle speed to the comely Queen Guinevere: 'Dear lady, let not this day's doings dismay thee at all. Such craft well becomes the Feast of Christmas; gamings and interludes and laughing and singing and carollings of knights and ladies. And now can I dress myself for meat, for a wondrous adventure have I seen.' He glanced at Sir Gawain and said, 'Now, sir, hang up thine axe; hewing enough has it done for today.' Then they hung it up over the dai's at the back of the high seat, that all men might look upon the marvel of it and truly tell the wonder of it. Then went these two, the king and the good knight, to the table, and brave men served them, double of all dainties, with all manner of meat and minstrelsy. In good weal they passed the day, but it came to an end, and night

>was near.
'Now, Sir Gawain, be sure,
Turn not away for fear
>From this grim adventure
That thou hast promised here.'

Canto the second

I

NOW, this was the first adventure Arthur had in the year that was young; he yearned for some great show, though no words were spoken as they went to their seats. And, moreover, they had in hand quite enough to do. Sir Gawain was full glad to begin the games in the hall : it is no wonder, though heavy be the ending, and though men be merry-minded when drinking good wine, yet the year runneth rapidly and returneth it never. Full seldom agreeth the end thereof with the beginning. The Yuletide, too quickly it passed and the year that followed it. The seasons succeeded

each after the other. After Christmas came the crabbed Lenten season, when the folk eat fish and simple food. Then the weather of the world doth fight with winter. The cold doth vanish and the clouds uplift, and the rain falls upon fair fields in warm showers, and the flowers appear on the ground, and in the woodlands their garments are green. Birds are busy in building their nests, and boldly they sing because of the summer's soft solace that follows thereafter
>   on bank,
> And blossoms swell to blow
> In rows rich and rank,
>   And bird-notes sweet enow
> Are heard in woodlands dank.

II

AFTER the summer season of soft winds, when zephyrs are sighing over seeds and herbs, and the damp dews are dropping from the green leaves, then are they glad thereat, the living things that grow there waiting for the blissful blushing of the bright sun. Then hastens the harvest and hardens them right soon, and warns them before the coming of winter to wax full ripe. And the dust by the drought is driven about from the face of the fields, and it bloweth full high. And the fierce winds of the welkins wrestle with the sun. And the leaves of the trees fall to the ground, and grey is the grass that was green erewhile. Then all ripens and rots that grew up before. Thus quickly passeth the year in many yesterdays, and winter returneth will ye nill ye.

   Surely
 Till moon of Michaelmas
Was won with winter's surety.
  Then thinks Gawain, alas!
Of his sorrowful journey.

III

ET did he linger with Arthur until All Hallows Day. And on that festival Arthur made a feast for the sake of Sir Gawain, with much rich revelling of the Round Table. And full comely knights and comely ladies were in great love-longing for Sir Gawain, though they made great mirth withal.

And many were jesting who yet were joyless, for that gentle knight. For after meat he sadly turned towards his uncle, and spake of his passing, and straightway he said, 'Now, my Life's Liege Lord, I ask thy leave. Thou knowest the cost of this matter, and careless am I of it, and to tell thee of it matters but a little. Tomorrow I am setting out to receive back the blow, and to seek the Green Knight as God shall direct me.' Then the best of all the burgesses banded together; Aywan and Errik and many others : Sir Doddinaual de Sauage, the Duke of Clarence, Launcelot, and Lyonel and Lucan the Good; Sir Bors and Sir Bedivere, great men both of them, and many other mighty lords, with Madoc de la Port. All this company of the court came near the king to counsel the knight; and their hearts were full of care, and great was the grief that grew in the hall that so worthy a man as Gawain should go on that journey a dreadful blow to endure and deal not one in return.

'For why?
The knight made aye good cheer,
'Why should I not defy
Destinies strong and dear;
What can man do but try?'

IV

E remained there that day, and dressed in the morning, and asked early for his arms, and they were all brought unto him. And first a carpet of tuly was spread on the floor, and much gold gleamed upon it. The strong man stepped forth and handled the steel, and donned a doublet of very costly Tarsian silk, and then a fair cap closed in above, and with fair fur was it bound inside. Then set they steel shoes upon the man's feet, and his legs they lapped in steel with lovely greaves and knee-pieces fastened thereunto and polished full brightly and fixed about his knees with knots of gold. Fair cuisses also cunningly covered his thighs, that were thick and brawny, and were tied with thongs. And then the woven bryny of bright steel rings enfolded the warrior over the fair stuff, and well burnished braces were upon both his arms, and good and gay elbow-pieces and plated gloves, and all the goodly gear that befitted such a knight, for
that tide,

With rich coat of armour,
Gold spurs he fixed with pride,
    Girt with a sword full sure,
And silk girths round his side.

V

S soon as he was fully armed, his trappings were noble, and the very least latchet or loop gleamed of gold. Thus accoutred, he heard Mass sung at the High Altar. Then he came to the king and to his court comrades, and lovingly took leave of lords and ladies, and they kissed him and commended him to Christ. By that time his horse, Gringolet, was geared and girt with a saddle, that gleamed full gaily with many golden fringes everywhere newly nailed and enriched for the business he had in hand. The horse's bridle was striped across and across, and bound with bright gold. The trappings of the horse's neck and of the proud skirts, the crupper and the covering,

accorded with the saddle, and were all bordered in rich red gold nails. Then he took hold of the helmet and hastily kissed it, and it was strongly stapled and stuffed within. It was high on his head, and hasped behind with a light kerchief of pleasaunce over the visor, and embroidered and bound with the best of gems on broad silken borders and with birds on the borders, such as painted parrots at their feeding, and with turtles and true-love knots intertwisted thickly, and it was as if many a maiden had been making it seven winters

> In the town.
> The circle was most of price
> That surrounded the crown;
> Of diamonds a device,
> And both were bright and brown.

VI

THEN they showed him the shield of shining gules and the pentangle painted with pure golden hues. He brandished it by the belt, and about his neck he cast it, that he was seemly and fair to look upon. And I am intent to tell you, though I may weary you

somewhat, why that pentangle belonged to that noble prince. It is a symbol that Solomon set up some while for betokening of truth, as its name doth show. For it is a figure that hath five points, and each line overlaps, and is locked in the other, and everywhere it is endless, and the English call it, as I hear, the endless knot. Therefore was it befitting this knight andhis clean armour. For Sir Gawain was known as a knight both good and true and faithful in five and many times five, and pure as gold, and void of all villany was he, and adorned with virtues
>
> in the mote,
> For the pentangle new
> He bears in shield and coat,
> And is a knight most true
> And gentle man, I wot.

VII

AND first he was found faultless in his five wits. Then he failed not in his five fingers. And all his trust on earth was in the five wounds suffered by Christ on the cross, as the creeds do tell us, so that when the knight was placed in the mêlée, his thought was ever upon them above all other things. And so it was that all his strength he found in the five joys that the fair Queen of Heaven had in her child. And for this cause it was that the knight had made to be painted her image in comely fashion on the greater half of his shield, so that when he looked upon it his valour never failed him. Now the fifth five that this knight excelled in were frankness and fellowship above all others, his cleanness and courtesy never were crooked, and compassion, that surpasseth all else. These five pure virtues were fixed in this knight more firmly than in any other. And all five

times were so joined in him that each one held to the other without any ending and fixed at five points, nor did they ever fail; for they were joined at no point nor sundered were they at all, nor could one find any end thereof at any corner when the games began or were gliding towards an ending. Therefore the knot was shaped on his strong shield, all with red gold upon red gules, called the pure pentangle among the people
of love.

Now geared is Gawain gay,
He brandished the lance he bore,
And bade them all good day,
And went forth evermore.

Now passed Sir Gawain on Gods behalf through the realms of Logres.

VIII

HE spurred his steed so strongly, and sprang forward on his way, that the stones struck fire as he rode. And all that saw that gallant knight sighed in their hearts. And each man, caring much for the comely one, said the same words to his neighbour, 'By Christ, it is scathe that he should be slain who is so noble of life. In faith it is not easy to find his fellow upon earth. Now, verily, to have wrought would have been wiser, or to have made yonder dear man a duke; a shining leader of men in the land he should be. This would have been better than that he should be broken to nought, and haled by an elvish man in arrogant pride. Whoever knew any king such counsel to take as knights who are cavilling at the Christmas games? 'Many were the warm tears that welled from their eyes when that seemly sire went forth from those dwellings

that day.
So he made no abode,
But quickly went his way;
Many a desert path he rode,
As I in book heard say.

IX

NOW passed Sir Gawain on God's behalf through the realms of Logres, though no game he thought it; and often alone he lingered at night-time when he sought in vain for the way that he longed for. No companion had he save his horse, nor no one but God to whom he might call by the way. And now he was nearing the north parts of Wales, with the Isle of Anglesea on the left. He fared over the fords along by the forelands. At the Holy head Hill he had the heights behind him in the wilderness of Wirral. Few dwelt there that loved either God or man with a good heart. And ever as he fared he would ask any that he met if they had ever heard speak of the Green Knight in any part thereabouts, or of the Green Chapel. All denied with a nay that ever in their lives they had known such a knight of such a hue

of green.
The way of the knight was strange;
By many a hillside, I ween,
His face gan oft to change,
Or ever the chapel was seen.

X

HE climbed many a cliff in strange countries, far removed from his friends in foreign parts he fared, and at each waterway that he passed over he found a foe before him, and a wonder, I trow, so terrible in appearance that to fight him he was forced; and many a marvel among the mountains he found, that it would be too tedious to tell the tenth part of what he found. He fought with dragons and wolves, and sometimes with madmen that dwelt among the rocks, and at other times with bulls and bears and boars, and with monsters that attacked him from the high mountain; and had he not been stiff and strong and serving the Lord, doubtless he had been done to death ere this. Fighting troubled him not so much, but the wintry weather was worse; when the clouds shed down upon him cold clear water, freezing ere it reached the fallow earth. Almost slain by the cold sleet, he slept in his harness, more nights than enough amidst the naked rocks where the cold burn ran by clattering from the crest, and hanging high above his head in hard icicles. Thus in perils and many a painful plight this knight wended his way until Christmas Eve arrived.

The knight that tide,
To Mary he cried,
To show him where to ride
Till some shelter he spied.

XI

N the morning he rode merrily by a mountain, through a full deep and wondrous wild forest; high hills were on each side, and woods of huge and hoary oaks, a hundred of them together, beneath him. The hazel and the hawthorn were trailing together with rough, ragged moss spread on all sides. Sorrowful birds sang on the bare twigs and piped piteously through pain of the cold. Upon Gringolet the man glided underneath them, all alone, through mud and mire, careful of his labour, lest he should be too late to see the service of his Lord, who on that night was born of a maiden our strife to be ending. Therefore, sighing, he said, 'I beseech thee, O Lord, and Mary, our dearest and mildest mother, that ye would grant me some place of rest where I might hear the Mass and matins of this moon. Full meekly I ask it, and thereto I will say full soon my pater and ave

and creed.'

He rode as he prayed,
And cried for misdeed,
And sign of Cross made,
And said, 'Christ's Cross me speed.'

XII

SCARCELY had he thrice signed himself with the sign of the Cross, when he was ware of a castle in the wood, on an upland or hill embosomed in the foliage of many a burly monarch of the forest. It was the comeliest castle that ever a knight possessed, in the centre of a meadow, with a park all about it. A palace beautiful, and for more than two miles encircled by trees. The knight caught sight of this palace of refuge on one side, shimmering and shining through the sheeny oaks. He gently doffed his helmet, and gave high thanks to Jesus and St. Gilyan, who had both of them gently and courteously guided his footsteps and hearkened to his crying. 'Now,' quoth the knight, 'grant me good hostel.' When putting his gilt heels to Gringolet, fully by chance he chose the right path, and full soon it brought him to the end of the drawbridge
        at last.

The bridge was soon upraised,
The gates were shut so fast,
The walls were well appraised,
They feared not the wind's blast.

XIII

HE knight, on horseback, stood still on the side of the deep double ditch that led to the place. The wall of the castle was wondrously deep in the water, and rose up aloft a full great height and was built of hard hewn stone right up to the corbels, which were supported under the battlements in the very best fashion, and with watchtowers full gaily geared between, and with many a clear and lovely loophole; and that knight had never seen a better barbican. He beheld the great and high hall of the castle, and its towers builded between very thick trochets; 1 fair and wondrously big round towers were they, with carved capitals craftily fashioned; and he saw the chalk-white chimneys, not a few, above castellated roofs that shone all white. And so many painted pinnacles were there everywhere, among the castle battlements clustered so thickly, that it seemed as if they had been cut out of paper. The noble man thought it full fair as he rode forward, if by any chance he might come within the castle cloister and harbour in that hostel during that

>holy day.
>Then came when he did call,
>A porter full gay,
>And took stand on the wall,
>And hailed the knight alway.

XIV

'GOOD sir,' quoth Gawain, 'wilt thou go mine errand to the high lord of this place to crave of him for me a place of refuge?' 'By St. Peter,' quoth the porter, 'yea, surely I trow thou shall be welcome to stay as long as thou likest.' Soon after the porter came again, and with him were noble folk who had come to welcome the knight. They let down the great drawbridge, and joyfully went forth, and knelt down upon the cold earth to do honour to the same knight as it seemed worthy to them. And they swung the broad gate widely on its hinges, and he saluted them royally, and rode in over the bridge. And many a fellow held for him his saddle while he alighted, and full many strong men stabled his steed. Knights and squires then came down that they might bring him with joy into the hall. And when he doffed his helmet others enow hastened to receive it at his hand, and took from him his sword and his shield. Then saluted he full kindly each one of these noblemen, and many a proud man pressed forward to pay honour to that prince. And they led him, all clad as he was in his high weeds, into the hall, where a fair fire burned fiercely upon the hearth. Then the lord of that people came down from his chamber that he might receive honourably the knight in the hall, and he said, 'Thou art welcometo do as it liketh thee. All that thou findest here is thine own to do with it as thou wiliest and

    to possess.'
 'Great thanks,' quoth Gawain.
'May Christ always thee bless.'
  As fellows that were fain,
Each the other gave press.

XV

AWAIN glanced at the man who thus gave him good greeting, and thought him a mighty man that was master of the castle, a huge fellow for the nonce and of great age. Broad and bright was his beard, and of beaver hue, and strong and stiff was he in his stride and stalwart in shanks, and his face was fierce as fire, and of speech was he free, and well he seemed, forsooth, to our knight to hold landlordship of a free, good people. The lord of the castle led him to a chamber, and speedily commanded that a page should wait upon him loyally. And at his bidding servants enow were at hand, who straightway brought him to a bright room, where the bedding was noble, with curtains of clean silk, with bright gold hems and full curious and comely canopies and embroidered above with bright linen lawns, and the curtains ran on ropes with red gold rings. Tapestries of Tuly and Tars were hanging on the walls, and on the floors carpets of the same

patterns. And then with merry speeches they took off his bryny and his gay clothing. And they brought him rich robes full readily, that he might choose the very best. And soon as he took them and was dressed therein, well did they become him. And in his flowing robes the knight seemed verily to each man there to be gay with beautiful colours. And his limbs under them were so lovely and shining that it seemed to them a comelier knight Christ never made
        for sight.
'Whence was he on earth?'
It seemed as though he might
        Be prince of peerless worth,
In field where fierce men fight!

XVI

A CHAIR richly embroidered, together with quaint cushions and hassocks, was placed for Sir Gawain before the chimney where a fire of charcoal was burning. And then a well-made mantle was cast upon his shoulders, and it was of brown linen and embroidered full richly and fair furred within with the finest of skins and with ermine lining, and the hood also. And thus richly arrayed, he sat in that chair, and as he warmed himself, speedily his good cheer quite returned to him. And then they set up a table on fair trestles, and they covered it with a snow-white cloth and set thereon sanat and salt-cellars and silver spoons. Then the knight gladly washed himself and went to his meat. And serving-men served him in seemly fashion, with several sorts of stews and sweets, with seasonings of the best, double fold, as was fitting, and many kinds of fish, some baked with bread, and some roasted on coals, some sodden, some stewed, and savoured with spices and, withal, with clever speeches that the knight liked well. A full noble feasting the man called it when those Athelings cheered him

                as friends.
    'This penance now you take,
And you shall make amends.'

    That knight much mirth 'gan make
For wine that to head wends.

XVII

THEN did they, in spare fashion and privately, put questions to that princely man, and he answered them courteously that he was a knight of the court of King Arthur, that rich and royal King of the Round Table, and that to him alone he owed fealty, and that it was Sir Gawain himself sitting there, and that he was come to keep that Christmas with them as it had happened. When the lord of the castle heard that he had him in his power at last, loud laughed he thereat, so lief was it to him, and all the men in that mote made much joy to be in his presence at that very time, since prowess and purest manners were ever to be found in his person, more than in all other men upon earth, and most honourable was he. Each man softly said to his fellow, 'Now shall we, as is fitting, see modes and manners and noble talking without a blemish, and what is fair in speech unsought we shall learn, since we have here this fine father of nurture. God has given us His goodly grace

forsooth, in that He granteth us to have so goodly a guest as Sir Gawain, when merry men of his breeding
> shall sing.
> Good manners now, I trow,
> This knight shall be bringing;
> > Who heareth him enow
> Shall learn of love talking.'

XVIII

HEN dinner was done, this noble man arose, and as night time was nearing, the chaplains were making their way to the chapel. Bells rang richly, as was right, to the proper evensong of that high feast. The lord and his lady also came down to the chapel, and the lady entered quaintly into a comely closet. Gawain glided in gaily full soon. The lord of the castle caught hold of the hem of his robe, and led him to a seat, and called him by name, and said he was of all men in the world the most welcome, and gave him great thanks, and they embraced each other, and all the time of the service they sat side by side. Then did the lady list to look on the

knight. Then came she from her closet with many fair maidens. Now her skin, and eke her flesh and her countenance, were the fairest of all, as she was also in form and colour and in all other virtues, and she was fairer even than Guinevere, as it seemed to Sir Gawain. And as he looked down the chancel upon that sweet lady he saw that another lady led her by the left hand, older than she was, an ancient as it seemed and high in honour, and nobles were about her. Very unlike to look upon were those two ladies, for if the young one was fair, yellow was that other one; rose red was the young one, rose red all over, whilst the other had rough and rolling wrinkled cheeks. The young one had kerchiefs with many fair pearls displayed upon her breast and her bright throat, shining sheenier than snow that falls on the hilltops; the other had a wrap on her neck folded over her black chin in milk-white veils; her forehead was folded in silks, lumped up and adorned with trifling jewels. Nothing was bare of that lady but her black eyebrows, her two eyes, her nose, and naked lips. And a sour sight were they to see, and strangely bleared. Men might say that in her a worshipful ancient lady
     was found.
 Her body was short and thick,
Her buttocks broad and round;
 A comelier one to pick
Was the lady she led on ground.

XIX

OW when Gawain glanced towards that gay lady, who looked so graciously, he took leave of the lord and went towards the ladies. He hailed the ancient one, and inclined himself full humbly. The lovelier of the two he took a little in his arms and kissed her in comely fashion, and addressed her courteously. They returned his greeting, and right soon he asked that he might be her servant. They took him between them, and talking together they led him to his chamber and towards the chimney corner, and they straightway asked for spices, which the pages brought full speedily, and winsome wine they brought with the spices. And the lord of the castle leapt aloft full often, for he intended that they should make mirth. He took off his hood right speedily, and hung it on a spear, and bade them win the worship thereof andso make the most mirth that Christmas tide. 'And I shall try, by my faith, to contend with the best ere I come short of it by help of my friends.' Thus doth that lord make sport with laughing words, that he might gladden Sir Gawain with games in the hall that night,

Till that it was tide,
That the king commanded light,
Sir Gawain no more doth bide,
But for bed him doth dight.

XX

N the morrow morn, when all men call to mind how the Lord was born to die for our destiny, joy waxed everywhere in the world for Christ's dear sake. So was it in that castle. And doughty men on the daïs served many a dainty mess at meal times. And the ancient lady sat in the highest seat on the daïs. And the lovely lord sat by her side, as I trow. Gawain and the gay lady sat together in the midst whilst the messes were served, and throughout all the hall the folk were served, each according to his rank. There was meat and mirth, and so much

joy that to tell thereof were much trouble to me, yet peradventure I may take the trouble. For I know that Gawain and the gay lady had great comfort of each other's company for the dear dalliance of their whispered words, and with clean and courteous talk, free from filth. And their playing surpassed of all princes
>> the game.
> And trumpets do blare,
And much sounding declaim;
>> Each of his own took care,
And they two did the same.

XXI

ND there were many blows struck for two days, and the third day came quickly enow. And gentle was the joy-making of St. John's Day, which was to be the last day of the games, the folk were thinking. On the grey morning a tournament was to be held. And, wondering, they awoke and drank wine, and carolling they danced

full doughtily. And at length, when it was late in the day, they took their leave, each strong man to wend on his way. Gawain bade them good day, and the good man of the house took him and led him to his own chamber beside the chimney-piece, and drawing him aside, thanked him dearly for the goodly worship he had given unto him in honouring his house as his guest and giving good cheer during the high feast. 'I trow,' said he, 'while I live, well worth will it be that Gawain was my guest at God's own feasting.' 'Grammercy.' said Sir Gawain, 'in good faith thine is the honour, not mine, and may the good God grant it unto thee. I am at thy service to do thy behest as it behoves me in high and low things
   by right.'

  The Lord was then full fain
Longer to hold that knight :
  To him answered Gawain,
In no way that he might.

XXII

THEN sought the lord of the castle to know full surely what doughty deed he had in hand at that dear season of the year, that he came forth so keenly to journey all alone from the court of the great King Arthur before the holly of Christmas was taken down in the city. 'Forsooth,' said the man, 'thou sayest well. A high and hasty errand it was that had me forth from the court. I am summoned forth to seek out a certain place, and I know not whither to wend to find it. And for all the land of Logres, so help me our Lord, I would not fail to find it by New Year's morning. Therefore I make this request of thee here that thou wilt truly tell me if ever thou hast heard tell where standeth the Green Chapel and the Green Knight that doth keep it. By statute there was made a covenant between us that if I might be still in the land of the living, I should meet him on that day at the Green Chapel. And it now wanteth but a little of that New Year, and I would more fain and gladlier look upon that man if God will than possess any good in all the world. By your leave, therefore, it behoves me to wend thither, as I have now for the business but barely three days. As fain would I fall dead as fail of my errand.' Then the lord laughing said, 'It behoves thee rather to linger here. For by the end of the time, I will show thee the way. Grieve thyself no more about the Green Chapel. For at least four days thou shalt be at ease in thy bedchamber. Then on the first of the New Year thou shalt ride forth towards that chapel in the morning and do as thou wilt.

>Meanwhile,
>Rest here till New Year's day,
>Then rise up without guile,
>Men shall set thee in the way
>It is not hence two mile.'

XXIII

THEN was Gawain right glad, and in gamesome mood he laughed and said, 'Now for this above all else I thank thee right heartily. Achieved will be my chance. I will dwell here meanwhile as thou wilt, and do as thou dost deem well.' Then the lord took him and set him at his side, and caused the ladies to be brought, so that they might be better pleased, though they had seemly solace in each other. And for love the lord spake many merry words, as though he scarce knew what he would say. Then he cried aloud and spake to the knight, 'Thou hast promised to do what I shall tell thee. Wilt thou do this behest that I bid thee at this time?' 'Yea sir, forsooth will I,' said the true man. 'While I bide in thy castle I am bound by thy behests.' 'Thou hast come,' quoth the lord, 'from a far country, and hast passed much waiting time with me, and hast gone short of sustenance and of sleep. I know it, forsooth. Thou shalt linger in thy sleeping-chamber at thine ease tomorrow morn, during the time of the Mass; then shalt thou wend to thy meat with my wife, and shalt sit at her side and comfort thee with her company till I return to the courtyard of the castle

   at the end.
  For I shall early rise
And a-hunting I shall wend.'
  Gawain takes his advice,
Bowing courtly to his friend.

XXIV

'UT further,' quoth that lord, 'we will make a covenant that what I win in the woodlands thine it shall be, and whatsoever fortune thou shalt achieve here shall be given by thee to me in exchange for my gift to thee. Swear soothly that we will make this exchange between us, whether hap be loss or gain to us.' 'By God,' quoth Sir Gawain, 'I grant thee thy word, and lief it is to me that thou dost list to make sport.' 'Let some one bring us wine,' said the lord of the castle,' for now this bargain is made between us'; and they both of them laughed and drank deep, and the lords and the ladies held dalliance together until night came. Then with many strange doings and fair words not a few, they stood still and spake softly, and kissed in comely fashion, and took their leave. And each was brought to his bed

attended by many a page and by flaming torches full soft.
>> To bed, ere they go out,
They recorded covenant oft.
>> The old lord of that rout
Could well hold sport aloft.

Canto the third.

I

FULL early before daybreak the folk that would go a-hunting rose up and called their grooms, and stirred them up to saddle the horses, gear up the trappings, and pack the bags, and dress them in noble array for riding. Then they leaped up lightly and seized the bridles, and each went the way he liked best. And the beloved lord of that land was not the last to appear. He was arrayed for riding with many a rider. And having heard the Mass he ate a sop hastily, and full readily he went forth to the bent field with bugle, before any daylight shone on the world. The lord and his nobles were upon high-stepping steeds.

Then the cunning huntsmen coupled the hounds, opened the kennel-doors, and called them out, and blew three bold, clear notes on the bugles. At this there was a baying and a very great barking, and the huntsmen tuined and whipped up the dogs. A hundred hunters of the best, as I have heard

>the word.
>To the trystings the trackers go,
>The hounds the hunters stirred;
>Because of the blasts they blow
>Great noise in the forest is heard.

II

T the first cry of the quest the quarry trembled with fear. The deer were driven in the dale, doting for dread. Then they hastened to the high lands, but hotly they were stopped at the trystings, where was great shouting. Harts with their high heads were let pass, and the bold bucks with their broad antlers. For the noble lord had forbidden that in the close season any man should molest the male deer. The hinds, however, were held back with a

Hi! and a cry, and the does with great din were harried to the deep valleys, and as they stumbled there was glancing of arrows, so that each that turned under the trees an arrow pierced him like the wind, and they boldly bit into the deer with full broad heads. So with braying and bleeding by the hillsides they died; and ever the hounds readily followed with a rush as the hunters on high horses hustled them forward with crashing cries, as though the very rocks had burst asunder. The deer that escaped the shooting of the shooters were all of them run down and pierced by the men on foot. They were harried at the high places and harassed at the waterways, for the huntsmen were such old hands at the low trysting-places and the greyhounds so strong that got at them that they seized them as quickly as a man might glance
    aside.
  The glad lord shouts 'abloy!'
Full oft 'gan fall and ride,
  And hunts that day with joy
Until the dark night tide.

III

THUS did the lord make sport by the borders of the lind wood whilst Gawain the good lay in bed at his ease until daylight fell athwart the walls. As he dozed there under full white canopies curtained about, he suddenly heard a slight noise at the door. He lifted up his head from under the clothes, and caught up a little the cover of the curtain, and looked warily thitherwards if he might find out what it was. And he saw the lady, the loveliest to behold, and she drew the door after her darkly and softly, and came towards the bed. Sir Gawain was covered with shame, and quickly laid himself down and made as though he were sleeping. And stepping softly, she stole to his bedside, cast up the curtain and stepped within it, and sat down on the side of the bed, and lingered there, wondrous long, watching for him to waken. The man lay hiding there a full long time, troubled in his conscience as to the meaning of this, for a marvel it seemed. Yet he said to himself, 'More

fitting it would be to speak to her and find out what she would.' Then he started up and turned towards her, and slowly opened his eyelids and looked wonderingly upon her, and crossed himself for greater safety that he might speak
full true.
With chin and cheek full sweet,
Both white and red of hue,
Lovingly 'gan she greet,
Her small lips laughing too.

IV

'GOOD morrow, Sir Gawain,' said the lady fair, 'full carelessly thou sleepest that one can thus creep into thy chamber. Now art thou taken unawares, and I shall bind thee in thy bed, of that be thou well assured.' Thus laughingly the lady uttered forth her jestings. 'And,' quoth Sir Gawain, 'Good morrow, gay lady; it will be well pleasing to me to be at thy service, and I yield myself thereto, and desire thy favour as must needs be.' Thus did he dally with her with full glad laughter. 'But wouldst thou, lovely lady, be so good as grant me leave to rise and thus to set free thy captive? for I would fain rise from this bed and put on my robes, so should I talk with thee with greater comfort.' 'Nay, forsooth, good sir,' said that sweet one. 'Thou shalt not rise from thy bed. I will give thee better counsel. I will cover thee up in thy bed and hold converse with my knight, whom I have taken prisoner, for I wis that thou art Sir Gawain, whom all the world doth worship wheresoever thou dost ride forth. Thy worth and thy courtesy are praised alike by lords and ladies and by all living. And now thou art here with me alone. My lord and his people are gone far away, and the other men are in bed asleep, and also my maids. The door is fast closed and secured by a strong bolt. So, since I have in this castle the man whom all love, no time will I be losing while it doth last,

   In address.
 Of me have thy will,
For thou shalt me possess.
 Thy servant I am still,
As is fitting, I confess.'

Stepping softly she stole to his bedside.

V

'IN good faith,' quoth Gawain, 'I think it would be gain for me were I not he of whom thou speakest, for to attain such worship as thou dost offer me herewith I wot well I am unworthy. By God, I should be glad, if it seemed good unto thee, to do thee service or pleasaunce in word or deed, and a pure joy it would be unto me.' 'By my faith, Sir Gawain,' quoth the gay lady, 'if I held lightly the price and the prowess that pleaseth all others, it would be but a little dainty. There are ladies enow that would be liefer to hold thee happily in their power as I have thee, and in dear dalliance to hear thee speak dainty words and thereby gain comfort and rid them of care, than all the guerdon or gold that they possess. And as I love the Lord who holdeth up heaven aloft, I have in my hands that which all desire through grace.'

> She made him so great cheer,
> That was so fair of face,
> With speeches pure, that peer
> Answered in each case.

VI

'MADAM,' quoth the merry man, 'may Mary bless thee! I have found thee, in good faith, noble and frank. Full many others did me courtesy, and the dainty that they dealt me was foolishness; but thy worship is that of one who knoweth nothing but good.' 'By Mary,' quoth the lady, 'I think otherwise, for were I worth all the wealth of women on earth, and all the wealth of the world were in my hand, were I to bargain and choose and take captive a lord, then no fellow on earth before thee would I choose, because of thy courtesy and beauty and good manners, and thy blitheness of mien, and because of what I have heard from thee and hold for the truth.' 'Well I wot,' quoth Gawain, 'thou hast chosen a better man than I am, yet am I proud of the price thou puttest upon me, and soberly as thy servant I hold thee as my sovereign, and thy knight I become, and may Christ requite thee.' Thus did they talk of many things till the midnoon was past. The lady seemed to be pleased therewith, and to love him. And Sir Gawain bore himself bravely. Yet the knight had in mind that though she were the fairest of ladies, there must be no love-making for him because of the loss that he was seeking

           eftsoon.

The blow he must abide,
And it must needs be done;
    The lady turned aside;
He grants her leave full soon.

VII

HEN she gave him good-day with a laughing glance, and standing there she caused him to wonder at the strength of her words. 'Now, he that speedeth all speech, yield us this sport, but I have it in my mind that thou art not Sir Gawain.' 'Wherefore?' quoth Sir Gawain, and afresh he asked her questions, fearing lest he had failed in his bearing

and manners. But the lady blessed him, and gave her reason. 'Since Gawain is fitly held to be so gallant and courteous, he could not so long have lingered lightly with a lady without craving a kiss for courtesy's sake and some little trifle at the end of his dalliance.' Then said Gawain, 'Let it be as thou dost wish. I will kiss if thou dost command, as befits a knight who fears to displease thee, so let there be an end to thy pleading.' With that she came near to him and caught him in her arms and bent down gracefully and kissed the knight, and they commended each other to Christ. Then she went out at the door without noise. Sir Gawain rose up readily, and making haste, called to his chamberlain and chose his dresses; and as soon as he was dressed went forth gaily to Mass, and then to meat, which had been courteously kept for him, and made merry till the moon rose,
    all day.
  No man did e'er make jest
With ladies so worthy and gay;
  Much pleasure they confessed
They had of him that day.

VIII

AND ever the lord of the land was busy with his sporting, hunting in holt and heath after the barren hinds, and by the setting of the sun there had been such a slaughter of does and of deer as was a wonder to behold. Then at last quickly flocked the folk together and fiercely made a quarry of the dead deer. And the noblest set to work with men enough; and, as is the custom, they cut up the quarry, and some of them burst open the breast, cutting the jointures with a sharp knife. Then they rent the limbs and the hide and took out the bowels, having lustily lanced it, dividing it deftly, and with their sharp knives sheared off the shoulders, haling them out by a little hole that the whole sides might be preserved. Then they broke the breast into two halves, and right quickly cut up the nombles, 1 and it was riven right up to the forks, and they readily lanced all the rib membranes and freed them from the backbone, all evenly to the haunch, and heaved up the part that is called the nombles

      by kind.

By the fork of the thighs,
The laps they lance behind;
To hew it in two devise,
By the backbone to unbind.

IX

THEN they hacked off both head and neck, and severed deftly the sides from the chine, and flung the fee of the crows into a grove hard by. Then they pierced both sides through at the ribs, and hung them by the houghs of the haunches. And each man took his share that fell to him, and they fed the hounds on the skins, and with the liver and the lights and the leathern paunches, with bread dipped in blood. Boldly they blew the horns, and the hounds bayed. Then having packed up the flesh they went homewards, blowing full strongly many bugle notes, so that by the time daylight had faded, home came the doughty men, to the comely

castle where Sir Gawain was biding,
full still.
Brightly the fire doth burn.
He greeteth with a will
The lord at his return;
With joy each one did thrill.

X

THEN the lord of the castle commanded the household to be marshalled, and the ladies to descend with their maidens, and the men in the hall to bring the spoils of the chase and spread them out before them. And Gawain, who was goodly in games, he called and showed him the tails of full fierce beasts, and the shining grease shorn from the ribs. 'How pay you this sporting?' quoth he; 'have I won the prize? Have I deserved hearty thanks because of my craft in hunting?' 'Yea, I trow,' cried Sir Gawain; 'here is the fairest venison I have seen for seven winters.' 'All this I give to thee, Sir Gawain,' quoth that other, 'according to our covenant it is thine own.' 'That is soothly said,' quoth Gawain, 'and that which I have won within this castle, I trow it is thine with my good will.' Then he clasps the fair neck of the lord in his arms and kisses him in comely fashion, 'Take thou thus what I have achieved; there is nothing else, or I would vouchsafe it to thee though it had been much greater.' 'Good it is,' said the good man, 'I say thee grammercy therefore. Now tell me boldly how thou didst win this wealth was it by thine own wit?' 'Nay,' quoth Gawain, 'that was not in our covenant; try me no further. I have given thee that which betides thee. Thou shouldst ask no more,

        I trow.'
They laugh and blithely talk
With words soft and low,
        Soon to supper they walk,
To dainties new enow.

XI

FTER supper they sat in the chimney corner, and oft were borne to them the costliest of wines, and often in their talking they agreed that on the morrow there should be the same covenant between them as before that whatever new chances betided them they would exchange them when they met in the evening. And they agreed to the covenant in the presence of all the household. And they drank together, pledging troth with many a good jest, and at the last took leave of each other lovingly. Each knight betook himself to his couch. Before the cackling cock had crowed three times, the lord leapt from his bed, and all the people who would go a-hunting. They went to Mass and then to meat, after which before day haddawned, they hied them to the woodlands
    to the chase.
  With high hunt and horns
They pass the plain apace,
    Uncoupled among the thorns
The hounds did race.

XII

OON they called a quest by the side of a marsh. The hunters who first found it cheered on the hounds with words, and there was a great hallooing, and the hounds, hearing it, hastened thither quickly, forty of them at once, and fell fast to the scent. Then arose such a roaring of the gathered hounds that the rocks were ringing thereabouts. The hunters harried them with their horns, and all of the hounds swayed together between a pool in the wood, and a cliff, a rugged place it was where the rugged rock had fallen. The hounds went before and the hunters followed after. They surrounded the cliff, and with the bloodhounds marked the beast that was within. Then the hunters beat the bushes and sought to make the prey leap forth. Suddenly and fiercely he rushed athwart the huntsmen one of the fiercest of swine. A long time had he dwelt apart from the herd, and he was very old and tough and baleful, and one of the greatest of boars, and whenever he grunted many were fearful, for at the very first thrust he hurled three men to the earth and caused many to fall back without further hurt. And they hallooed full high, with 'Hay! hay!' and hotly blew their horns; and merry were both hounds and hunters who hastened after the boar with boastful noises.

And why?
Full oft he bides the bay,
The hounds he doth defy,
He maims the dogs, and they
Full piteously howl and cry.

XIII

THEN the shooters shot their arrows at him, and often they struck him, but their points failed to pierce his hide, and the barbs would not bite his forehead. The shaven arrow-shafts shivered in pieces wheresoever they struck him. But whenever the blows at all pierced his flesh, then, maddened, he burst forth on the hunters and hurt them hotly as he hied. And many grew timid and drew back somewhat. But the lord riding on a light horse often pierced him, as boldly on the bent-field he blew his bugle, and called them back as he rode through the dense thickets, pursuing the boar till the sun shifted westwards. Thus on this day did they drive the boar, while our lovely knight lay on his bed in rich apparel,

>all bright.
>The lady quickly hies
>To greet the gentle knight,
>Full early doth she rise
>To change him if she might.

XIV

HE came towards the curtain and gazed at the knight, and Sir Gawain welcomed her courteously at first, and the lady talked with him earnestly. Then she sat at his side and laughingly with loving glances she delivered her soul, 'Sir, if thou art Sir Gawain, it is, I think, passing strange that a knight who is so well disposed to gallantry should not be well versed in the customs of good company, for even if thou dost know them, thou dost cast them forth from thy mind and hast right soon forgotten what I taught thee by my talking yesterday.' 'What may that be? 'quoth the knight. ' I wot not what thou meanest. If soothly thou speakest, then truly the fault is mine own.' Then said the lady, 'Why, truly. I taught thee of kissing, and that when the face of a lady is known, thou shouldst quickly claim thy meed, and that this is becoming in a knight who uses courtesy.' Then quoth the doughty man, 'Have done, dear lady, for that I durst not do, lest I should be denied, for by thy refusal should I find out my mistake.' 'By my faith,' quoth that fair one, 'thou shalt not be denied, for thou art strong enough to constrain one if thou likest, if any were so villanous as to refusethee.' 'Yea, surely,' quoth Gawain, 'good is thy speech, but to threaten a lady is deemed ungallant in the landwhere I live, as also are all gifts given without good will. I am at your service to kiss when thou likest. Thou mayest take it or leave it when it pleaseth thee,

in space
The lady bendeth low,
And comely kisses his face,
Much love-talk doth flow
Of love's joy and grace.

XV

'I WOULD be knowing from thee,' said that dear lady, 'an you were not wroth thereat, how it cometh to pass that thou who art so young and active, so courteous and so knightly as thou art known to be, and so given to chivalry, which is the most praiseworthy of all things, and so well versed in the loyal sport of love and in the science of arms, art yet so slow in lovemaking. For of all the achievements of true knights, this of lovemaking is the chiefest, and for their leal loves their lives they adventure, and endure doleful dintings, and have avenged them by their valour and delivered them from care, and have brought bliss into many a bower, and many a fine favour have bestowed; and yet thou, who art the comeliest knight of the age, and thy praise is spread abroad everywhere, hast had me sitting by thy side several times, and hast not spoken a single gentle word such as lovers do speak and such as belongeth to love,

neither little nor great; and thou who art courteous and quaint in thy promisings oughtest eagerly to teach a young thing some tokens of true love's craft. Why art thou backward who canst boast of praises, unless it is that thou deemest me too dull to hearken to thy dalliance?
>   For shame
>   Alone I come here and sit
> To learn of thee some game;
>   O teach me of thy wit
> While my lord is from home.'

XVI

'IN good faith,' quoth Sir Gawain, 'God give you good, great is this good glee of thine, and easeful is it to me that so worthy a lady as thou art shouldst come hither to me and trouble thyself about so poor a man, and play in any such fashion; but it would be, as I think, a manifold folly for me to take the trouble to expound true love, and tales of arms, to one who, as I wot well, hath more sleight in that art than a hundred men such as I am, or ever shall be, as long as I live upon earth. As far as I am able I

would work thy will, as I am beholden to do, and I would evermore be thy servant as save me the good Lord.' Thus did she tempt him often to wrong-doing according to her evil thought, but so well did he defend himself that of no fault seemed he guilty, nor was there evil wrought by either of them,
    but bliss.
  They laughed and played that day;
At last she gave him kiss,
  And then she went her way,
And took her leave, I wis.

XVII

THEN arose the knight, and betook him to Mass, after which breakfast was joyfully served, and Sir Gawain played with the lady all that day. But over the country the lord was riding following the mischievous boar by steep hillsides, and the beast bit the backs of his hounds in two. There he bode at bay till the bowmen broke in upon him and caused him to utter a cry as the arrows fell fleet upon him when the folk gathered about him. But yet he made the

stoutest-hearted to start, until at the last he was so weary that he could not run any longer, but as quickly as he could he gained a hole in a hillock near a rock at the side of a brook. He set himself with his back to the hillock and began to scratch, and full loathsome was his foaming at the mouth, and about his white tusks, and all the men who stood by him were a-weary, but at some distance were they, for near him none durst
aspire.
He had hurt so many before
That no man did desire
To be torn by his tusks any more,
For his brain was fiercely on fire.

XVIII

HEN came the lord of that rout himself and reined up his steed, and saw the boar at bay beside his men. He alighted in graceful fashion, and left his courser in charge, brandished forth a glittering sword and strode along with huge strides, crossed by the fording where the fierce beast was biding, who was ware of the weapon in his hand; then he heaved highly his bristles and so hotly he breathed that many of his men went

and stood before their lord, lest a worse fate should befall him. The boar made so great a rush for him that both he and the lord fell in a heap, in a place where the water rushed rapidly; but the boar had the worst of it, for the man marked him well as they met, and set his sword in the pit of the beast's stomach, even up to the hilt, so as to rive his heart; and the boar, snarling, gave up the struggle as he fell down in the water
on his knees.

A hundred hounds and more
Fiercely did him seize;
Men brought him to the shore,
And death gave him release.

XIX

HEN furious was the blast blown upon many a horn, and high hallooing on the part of the men, and the hounds bayed the beast as the masters of that dangerous chase did urge them on. Then one who was wise in woodcraft began to unlace this lovely boar. First he hewed off his head and set it on high, then he roughly rent him by the back and tore out his entrails, and burnt

them on hot coals, and rewarded his hounds with bread blended therewith; then he cut out the brawn in bright broad shields, and had out the hastlets, the two halves of which, all whole, he hung upon a strong pole. Then they made for home at a swinging pace, with the boar as their trophy, and the boar's head was borne before the knight who had fared into the ford so valiant
and strong.

He saw Sir Gawain in hall,
And the time it seemed full long;
He came when he did call
To take what to him did belong.

XX

HEN the lord saw Sir Gawain he greeted him with loud mirth and spake words of solace to him. Then he sent for the ladies and gathered the household; he showed to them the shields of the boar, and told them of his length and breadth and height, and of the boar's fierceness, and of the fight in the wood with the wild boar. Then Sir Gawain full comely commended his deeds, and praised him at great price, and said that never before had he seen such a brawn of a beast nor such sides of a boar. Then the gentle man handled the huge head and praised it. 'Now, Gawain,' quoth this good man, 'this game is thine own, as by our fast and fair covenant it was agreed.' 'True it is,' said that other, 'all that I have gained I will give it to thee by my troth.' Then he caught the lord about the neck and gently kissed him, and eftsoons he kissed him again. 'Now are we quits,' quoth the lord, 'this eventide of all the covenants we made since I came hither.'

'I trow
By St. Giles,' said the knight,
'Thou art the luckiest I know,
Great in gains thou art this night,
And a rich man thou dost grow.'

XXI

HEN they set up the tables, and cast cloths upon them, and the serving-men fixed flaming torches on the walls and set out the feast, and there was much mirth and glee in that hall, and many a stalwart man sang merry songs in many a wise during supper and afterwards, such as new carols of Christmas, with all sorts of good-mannered jesting that one may think of. And ever our lovely knight sat by the lady, and in seemly wise she bore herself towards him, and gentle was her bearing, that she might please so stalwart a man, so that he greatly marvelled thereat, and was wroth with himself. Yet would he not, because of his high lineage, make any return thereto, but dealt with her with care, howsoever things went.

> At last,
> When they had played in hall
> As long as their strength did last,
> To chamber he gave them call,
> And to the fireplace they passed.

XXII

AND there they drank each other's health and passed away the time, and the lord proffered to make the same covenant together for New Year's Eve. But the knight craved leave to depart on the morrow. For the time was drawing near when he should go. But the lord hindered him from going, and constrained him to bide a little longer, and said, 'As I am a true man, I give my troth that thou shalt arrive at the Green Chapel on New Year's morn long before prime,

that thou mayest perform thine oath. Therefore rest thou in thy bed and take thine ease while I shall hunt in the woods and keep the covenant between us and exchange our gains on my return hither. For I have proved thee twice and found thee faithful, now for the third time let us think on the morrow and make merry while we may, and be mindful of joy, for loss cometh when it will.' Sir Gawain readily consented thereto, and lingered a little longer, and they drank together and went to their rest
>	with light.
Sir Gawain lies and sleeps
Full still and soft all night,
>	The lord, that woodcraft keeps,
Full early he was dight.

XXIII

AFTER the Mass the lord and his men ate a hasty meal. Merry was the morn. He asked for his horse, and all his company whose duty it was to follow him were ready on their chargers before the hall gates. Wondrous fair was the world, for the hoar frost was on the ground. Ruddy and red the sun rose among the mists, and full clear cast aside the clouds of the welkin. The hunters dispersed themselves by the side of a wood, and the rocks and the trees rang with the noise of the horns. Some of the hunters fell in with the scent where the fox was biding, and oft they tracked and tracked across in wily fashion. One of the hounds took up the cry, and the hunters called him, and the others fell thereto panting hard and close together. They ran forth in a rabble right on his track. The fox ran on in front, and they found him at length and followed hard after him, and savagely they scolded him with an angry noise. He tricked them, and made quick turns in many a rough woodland, and dodged in and out, and sometimes would pause to listen by many a hedgerow. At length he leapt over a quickset hedge by the side of a little ditch, and then stole out stealthily by a rugged path, and tried to escape the hounds. Then, ere he knew it, he came suddenly upon one of the stations, where three hounds fiercely set upon him at once.

     All grey
     He quickly turned again,
And strongly sprang astray
     With all the woe and pain
To the wood he turned away.

XXIV

THEN truly it was fine sport to listen to the hounds when, all crowded together, they came upon him, and such curses were flung at him as though the clustering cliffs had clattered down in heaps. And as the huntsmen met him, they hallooed together with loud and snarling words. And they threatened him, and called him a thief, and ever the hounds were at his tail that he might not tarry a moment, and often as he ran on they rushed at him, and often they rolled over and over. So wily was Reynard. And oft he led them astray in this fashion over and under and amidst the mountains, while the gentle knight at home was sleeping within the comely curtains on that cold morning. But the lady could not sleep for love thinking, lest the purpose in her heart so firmly fixed should suffer harm. But she rose up quickly and ran to his chamber, dressed in a merry mantle furred and lined with the purest of skins, with no hues of gold her head adorning, but with precious stones

twined about her hair in clusters of twenty. And her face and her throat were all naked, and eke her breast before and behind. She came within the chamber, and closed it after her, flung wide open the window, and called to the knight, and thus greeted him with raillery and rich words, and

       with cheer.
 'Ah, man, how canst thou sleep?
The morning is so clear.'
  He was in drowsing deep,
And yet her words did hear.

XXV

UT the knight was sunk in fitful and dreamy slumbers, as if in the grip of sad thinking how that on that very day destiny would dight him his Weird, 1 when he should meet the Green Knight at his chapel and receive from him the blow without further words. But when that comely knight recovered his wits, he swung suddenly out of dreams and answered in haste. The lovely lady came towards

him laughing sweetly, and bending over his fair face she kissed him. And he welcomed her worthily, with a pleasant smile. For he saw her so gloriously and gaily attired, so faultless in her features, and of such a fine complexion, that a strong and welling joy warmed his heart. And straight they smote forth mirth and smiles; yet all was pure bliss, and no more than they felt within them
>				was right.
> The words they said were good,
> And their joy was fair and light;
>				Great peril between them stood,
> But Mary guarded her knight.

XXVI

FOR verily the worthy Prince bore himself as a victor; for she proffered herself to him so earnestly that it behoved him either to take her love or to refuse it in uncourteous fashion. He cared much for his courtesy, lest he should prove himself craven-hearted, and yet much more for the mischief that would follow were he to commit sin and betray the lord who was his host in that castle. 'God shield us,' said he, 'this shall not befall us,' and with spare love, laughing, he received all the words of choice that fell from her lips. And the lady said, 'Thou dost deserve great blame if thou lovest me not who am wounded in heart more than all else in the world; but perchance it is because thou hast a mistress that thou lovest better than thou lovest me, and holdest thy troth to her, and wouldst not lose her, as I trow. And now do thou tell me that truly, I pray thee; for the sake of all the true love in the world, hide it not from me

    through guile.'
  The knight said, 'By St. John,'
And softly he did smile,
    'In faith I have not one,
Nor none will have the while.'

Then he made a clean shrift

XXVII

'THAT word,' quoth she, 'is the worst of all. I am answered forsooth, and sore wounded am I. Kiss me now comely, and I will hie me hence. I can only mourn in the world as lovers do.'
Then, sighing, she stooped down and said as she stood there, 'Now, dear one, at my passing do me this ease; give me some little token, if it be only thy glove, that I may think on thee and thus lessen my grief.' 'Now I wot,' said the knight, 'I would that I had here the dearest thing I possess in the world, for thou hast, forsooth, deserved wondrous oft and rightly greater reward than I could ever bestow; but to bestow upon you some love-token, that would avail but little. For it would be a stain upon your honour at this time that Gawain should give you a glove as a reward, for I am come hither on the most unheard-of errand upon earth, and have no men or baggage with things of value for every man must bide his fate, whether of sorrow
or gall.'

'Nay, knight of high degree,'
Quoth the lady fair and tall,
　'Though nought thou givest me,
I'd yield to thee my all.'

XXVIII

HE gave him a rich ring of red gold, with a glittering stone standing out therefrom, from which shone forth blushing beams as of the bright sun; and surely it was of very great price. But the knight refused it, and readily he said, 'I will take no gift from thee at this time. I have none to offer thee in return, and none will I take.' She pressed it upon him, but he would none of it, and swiftly swore his sooth that he would not take it; and very sorrowful was she, and said, 'If thou refusest my ring because it seems to thee too rich a present, and thou wouldst not be so deeply beholden to me, I will give thee my girdle, for that is of less value.' She caught hold of a circlet of lace that girdled her sides and was fastened to her kirtle under the white mantle, and it was geared with green silk and shapen with gold and all embroidered with finger-work. She offered it to the knight, and blithely she besought him to accept it, though of little worth it were. But he said that he would not take it in no wise, neither gold nor treasure as God sent him grace, that he might achieve the event that he had chosen in coming there. 'And therefore I pray thee, be not displeased, and cease from this business, for I can never consent to thy request, therefore

>   do not rue;
> Dear debt to thee is mine
> As thy courtesy's due,
>   And ever in fair and fine
> I am thy servant true.'

XXIX

'OW dost thou refuse this silk girdle,' said the lady, 'for simple it is in itself and of little worth it seems. But whoso knew the virtues that are knit therein, he would appraise it at greater price, per-adventure. For whatsoever man is girded with this green lace while he has it secretly fastened about his body, there is no man under heaven that could hew him asunder. He could not be slain by any sleight or trick in the world.' Then the knight set himself to thinking, and it came into his heart that such a girdle would be a jewel in the jeopardy to which he was pledged in going to the Green Chapel to receive the deadly blow; and if he should slip and be in danger of death it would be a noble sleight of defence. Then he endured her chiding, and let her speak, and she thrust the belt upon him quickly, and he took it from her as she gave it with good will and besought him for her sake never to

reveal it, but to loyally hide it from her lord. The knight agreed thereto, and swore that no man should ever know it save they two, as she
did crave.
Great thanks he gave that day
With heart and mind so grave.
The third time, as I say,
She kissed that knight so brave.

XXX

THEN she took her leave, for there was no more love-play to be gained from the knight. As soon as she had gone, Sir Gawain dressed himself right soon and arrayed himself in noble garments and hid away the love-lace the lady had given him, where he could easily find it at need. Then first he went to the chapel of the castle and found out the priest, and prayed for absolution and that he would show to him a better way to save his soul when he should go thence. Then he made a clean shrift, and confessed his misdeeds both great and small, and sought for mercy. And the priest absolved him and gave him such cleanness as

though on the morrow doomsday should dawn.
Then he made himself so merry among the noble
ladies with comely carols and all kinds of joy as
never before or since that day, until the dark
night came
>>with bliss.
>Each one had dainty more
Of him and said, I wis,
>>That so merry he ne'er was before,
Since thither he came, ere this.

XXXI

ND he lingered there, where love was his portion. And all the time the lord was on the land leading his men, and he had killed the fox that he had followed so long, as he leapt over a hedge to spy upon the shrewd fellow. For there, as he heard the hounds that were hard upon him, Reynard came running through a rough grove, and all the rabble racing at his heels. The lord was ware of the fox, and warily he waited for him, and brandished forth the bright sword, and made a cast at him, whereat he flinched and should have retreated, but a hound rushed at him e'en before he could escape, and right in front of the feet of the horse they all fell upon him and worried the wily fellow to death with a loud noise. The lord alighted quickly, and soon caught hold of him and tore him out of the mouths of the dogs, and held him high above his head, hallooing the while, and many a brave hound bayed at him there. The hunters hied thither, blowing a recheat on their horns till they saw the knight, and by the time that his noble company were come up, all that bore bugles blew at the same time, and those who had no horns raised a great halloo! It was the merriest meet ever heard of, and the greatest noise ever made for the soul of a fox.

    With jest
 The hounds they did reward,
Their heads they then caressed,
   And then they took Reynard
And straightway him undressed.

XXXII

AND forthwith they made for home, blowing full stoutly on their loud horns, for night was drawing near. And at length the lord alighted at his beloved homestead, and found the fire on the floor and the knight beside it. Sir Gawain the good made merry with them all, for among the ladies he had much joy for love. He wore a fine blue linen mantle, that reached down to the ground, and his surcoat suited him well, for it was soft furred, and a hood of that ilk hung on his shoulder, and both were blended with fur. The lord met this good man in the midst of the hall, and greeted him gaily, and the knight spake goodly words: 'I will be the first to fulfil our covenant that we plighted together when the drink was not lacking.' Then he embraced the lord and kissed him three times as gravely and carefully as he

could. 'By Christ,' said the lord, 'thou hast had great joy in achieving such treasures, and thy bargain was a good one.' 'Yea then, no matter the bargain,' said that other, 'quickly is given the bargain I drove.' 'Marry,' quoth the lord, 'my prize is coming on after me, for all the day I have been hunting and nought have I gotten but this foul fox; and the devil take him, and indeed it is a poor return to make for such precious gifts as thou hast given me in three such kisses
   so good.'
 'Enough,' said Sir Gawain,
'I thank thee by the rood,'
  And how the fox was slain
He told him as they stood.

XXXIII

THEN with mirth and minstrelsy, and with meats at their will, they made as merry as any men could, and the ladies laughed merrily, and there were spoken many jesting words. And Gawain and the good man were both of them so glad that they were in danger of losing their heads or of becoming drunken. So great was the revelry in the hall until it was time to separate and retire to their beds. Then most humbly did the knight take leave of the lord, and in fair fashion he thanked him. 'May the High King bless thee for the wondrous sojourn I have had here in thy castle at this high feast. I pray thee to grant me one of thy men if thou wilt to show me, as thou didst promise, the way to the Green Chapel, so God will suffer me to endure on New Year's Day the destiny appointed me.' 'In good faith,' said the lord, 'with a right good will all that ever I promised thee I will hold to my reed.' Then he assigned him a servant to set him in the way and conduct him by the downs that he might suffer no hurt in going through the forests, and fare forth in gainly fashion,

                and live.
     The lord then thanked Gawain,
Such worship he would him give,
        And of the ladies twain
The knight then took his leave.

XXXIV

WITH courteous kisses he took leave of them all and gave them great thanks, and received their thanks in return. Then they entrusted him to Christ, and heaved deep sighs as he passed out from their midst, and each man that he met he gave him thanks for service and solace and the great pains they had taken, especially those who had done him personal service. And each man was sore troubled at parting with him with whom they had dwelt so worthily. Then with flaming torches they led him to his chamber, and blithely brought him to rest in his bed. I dare not say that he slept soundly, for of the morn he had much
>of thought.
>Let him lie there still,
>He is near that which he sought,
>>An ye will awhile be still
>I will tell you how he wrought.

Canto the fourth.

I

NOW drew near the New Year as the night waned and the darkness passed away as God doth bid. But wild weather of the world came out of the wakening day, and clouds cast down cold upon the earth, and there was enough of the north in the weather to vex the naked. And snow fell sharply and covered the wilds. The whistling wind rushed down from the heights, and there were great drifts in the dales. And as the knight lay in his bed he listened to the storm, and though he locked his eyelids, full little he slept, and he heard the crowing of each cock in turn. Ere the day dawned he dressed himself by the light of a lamp that gleamed in his chamber. He called to his servant, and quickly he answered him, and he bade him bring in his cuirass and his saddle, and he rose up forthwith and fetched the riding-apparel, and prepared Sir Gawain for his journey in great wise. First he clad him in his clothes, that he might ward off the cold, and then in his other harness that had been faithfully guarded. His coats of mail and his armour-plate all shone with burnishing, and the rings of his rich coat of mail were cleansed of all rust, and were all fresh as at first, and he was fain to thank

        him there.
  Of the armour every piece
He had wiped clean and fair,
    As no warrior's in Greece.
He asked for his steed so rare.

II

ND while he was then being decked out in these rich weeds, his coat with the badge of noble deeds, adorned as it was with stones of virtue upon velvet and bound with embroidered seams and fair furred within with costly furs, yet forgot he not the lace girdle, the lady's gift for his protection. When he had belted his sword upon his smooth haunches he wound the love-token round and round about him, and he quickly folded the gay girdle of green silk about his loins over the rich and royal red cloth. But he wore not this rich girdle for its great price, nor for pride of polished pendants, or because gold glittered and gleamed upon it, but to save himself when it behoved him to suffer and to bide bale without debate and to beware of the sword

     or blow.
  And then the bold knight down
From that fair castle doth go,
    All that household of renown
He thanketh them, I trow.

III

HEN his fine and huge horse Gringolet was made ready. He had been well cared for, and was proud and eager for galloping. Sir Gawain went up to him and looked in his face. Then he solemnly addressed the company, and swore, 'Here indeed is a well-mannered and courteous household, and may the lord who maintains them havegreat joy. And may love betide the dear lady of the house all her life. And when they cherish their guests and do honour to them, may the High Lord that wields heaven on high bless them and you all; and if I live long enough I will grant you some meed for your services.' Then stepped he into the stirrups and mounted his horse, and his servant handed him his shield, which he received on his shoulder, and then goading Gringolet with his golden spurs, he stood there no longer, but struck sparks from the stones, and the horse
    did prance.
  His man on horse was then

That bore his spear and lance,
>   'This castle to Christ I ken
> Oweth its good chance.'

IV

HEN the bridge was let down, and the broad gates were flung open, both halves of them. The knight crossed himself as he passed the threshold, and praised the porter, and knelt before the prince of that castle and bade him good day, and went on his way with his one servant who was to show him the path to that sorrowful place where he was doomed to receive the rueful blow. They took their way by hills where the boughs of the trees were bare, and they climbed up by cliffs where the frost was clinging. The clouds did not fling down the snow, but gloomy was it beneath. The moor was muggy with mist, and the snow melted on the mountains, and each hill had a cap or mantle of fog, and brooks boiled among the rocks, dashing white on the shores as they rushed downwards, and lonesome was the way as they

went by the woodlands until the time came for the sun to rise
>that tide.
They rode o'er a hill full high,
The white snow lay beside;
>The man who rode him by
Bade his master abide.

V

'FOR hither,' said the man, 'I have brought thee at this time, and now thou art not far from that famous place about which thou hast so specially asked so many questions. But soothly I will tell thee, since I know thee and thou art one among ten thousand, and I love thee well, that wouldst thou take my counsel it would be better for thee; for the place towards which thou dost press forward is held to be full perilous, for there dwells in that waste one of the worst upon earth. And he is strong and stern, and loves to deal great blows, and greater is he than any man in the world, and his body bigger than the best four knights that are in the house of King Arthur, Hector, or any others. And such chance he achieves at the Green Chapel that

none passes that place, though he be proud in his armour, but that he deals them a death-blow by a stroke of his hand. For pitiless is he, and shows no mercy. For whosoever rides past the chapel he thinks it as good to kill him as to remain alive himself, be he churl or chaplain, monk or mass-priest. Therefore I say to thee, forsooth, as thou dost sit in the saddle, if thou comest there, thou shalt be killed, believe thou that, forsooth, though thou hadst twenty lives
>to spend.
He has dwelt here of yore;
Do not thither wend,
>Against his dintings sore
Thou mayest not thee defend.'

VI

'FOR thy welfare, Sir Gawain, let him alone, and gang some other gait, for God's dear sake. Go where Christ may speed thee, and I will hie me home again; and further I promise thee on my oath, by God and all His good saints, as help me, God and Our Lady and others, that I will keep thy secret and say not

a word that ever thou didst turn back from thy quest.' 'Grammercy,' quoth Gawain, 'well may it be with thee for that thou desirest my good, and wouldst loyally keep a secret, as I believe thou wouldst verily, but didst thou keep it never so truly, were I to turn away for fear as thou dost bid me, a coward knight I should show myself and without excuse. Nay, but I will to the chapel, come what come may, and deal with that fellow as I list, and as Weird doth like, be it for weal
or woe.
Though he be fierce to yield,
And deal a deadly blow,
My God can full well shield
His servant from the foe.'

VII

'MARRY,' quoth that other, 'now thou hast said that thou wilt thrust thyself into such danger, and it listeth thee to lose thy life, I will not hinder thee. Set then thy helmet on thy head, and thy spear in thy hand, and ride down the path by the side of yonder rock till thou shalt come to the bottom of the rugged valley; then take a look round on thy left hand

and thou shalt see in the valley the very chapel that thou seekest and the burly fellow that keepeth it. Now fare thee well, and God bless thee, Gawain the noble. For all the gold in the world I would not wend with thee nor bear thee company through this valley a single inch farther.' Then the man turned his horse round in the wood, put his spurs to sides as hard as he could, and galloped over the land, leaving the knight alone.

'By God's self,' quoth Gawain,
I will neither weep nor groan;
To do His will I am full fain,
He will deliver me full soon.'

VIII

HEN spurred he Gringolet, and betook himself along the path by the side of a wood, and rode over a rough hill into the valley. And he lingered there some time, and a wild place he thought it, for he saw no resting-place, but only high hills on both sides, and rough, rugged rocks and huge boulders, and the hill shadows seemed desolating to him. Then he drew up his horse, and it seemed wondrous strange to him that he saw not the Green Chapel on any side. At length a little way off he caught sight of a round hillock by the side of a brook, and there was a ford across the brook, and the water therein bubbled as though it were boiling. The knight caught up the reins and came to the hill, alighted, and tied up the reins to the rugged branch of a tree.

Then he went to the hill and walked round about it, debating within himself what place it might be. It had a hole at the end and on either side, and it was overgrown with tufts of grass and was all round and hollow within. He thought it nought but an old cave or a crevice. Within and about it there seemed to be
   a spell.
  'Ah lord,' quoth the gentle knight,
'Is this the green chapel?
  Here truly at midnight
Might the devil his matins tell.'

IX

'OW,' said Sir Gawain, 'this is a desert place, I trow. This oratory is loathsome, overgrown as it is with weeds, and well it befitteth that fellow clad in green, for his devotion to the devil. Now in my five wits I ween it is the very devil himself who has made this tryst with me, that he may destroy me. This is a chapel of ill-luck, and the most accursed kirk that I have ever seen, and may ill luck befall it.'
With his helmet high on his head and lance in hand, he wandered up to that rocky dwelling. Then came there from a rock in that high hill beyond the brook a wondrous strange noise, and it clattered among the cliffs as though it would cleave them asunder, as though one were grinding a scythe upon a grindstone, and it made a whirring sound like water in a mill, and rushed and sang out and was terrible to hear.
'By God Himself,' said Gawain, 'that is the noise of armour which is being made ready for that fellow wherewith he may come forth to meet me
    by rote.
  Let God work me woe.

It helpeth me not a mote,
> My life though I forgo,
No noise shall make me dote.'

X

HEN in a loud voice the knight 'gan call, 'Who dwells in this place and would hold parley with me? For now is good Sir Gawain in the right way at last, and if any man would have aught with him let him come hither quickly; now or never is his chance.' 'Tarry a moment,' quoth a voice on the hill above his head, 'and thou shalt receive all that I promised thee in right good time.' Thereupon he rushed forward at a great speed till he arrived near a crag and came whirling out of a hole in a corner of it with a fell weapon in his hand; and it was a new Danish axe with which to give the blow, with a huge piece of steel bent at the handle, and it was four feet long and filed at the grindstone, and it gleamed full brightly. It was the Green Knight, dressed as at their first meeting, the same in face and legs, looks, and beard, save that he went on foot. When he reached the water he

would not wade therein, but hopped over on his axe and strode boldly forward over
the snow.

Sir Gawain the knight 'gan meet,
To him he bowed not low;
The other said, 'Now, my sweet,
The tryst thou keepest, I trow?'

XI

'GAWAIN,' quoth the Green Knight, 'may God protect thee. I wis thou art welcome to my place, and thou hast kept thy promise as befitteth a true man. Thou knowest the covenant between us made how a twelvemonth ago thou didst take that which befell thee and I was to be quits with thee on this New Year's Day. We are alone verily in this valley; there are no knights here to separate us. Doff thy helmet and take thy pay, and make no more ado than I did when thou didst whip off my head at one blow.'

'Nay, by the most high God,' said Gawain, 'so I have spirit I grudge thee not thy will for any mischief that may befall me; but I stand here for thy stroke, and do not deny thee thy will anywhere.'

Down he bent his head,
And showed his neck all bare.
There was no sign of dread,
Or that he would not dare.

XII

THEN the Green Knight gat himself ready quickly, and gathered up his grim weapon with which to smite Sir Gawain, and with all the strength of his body he raised it aloft and made a feint of destroying him and drove it downwards as though he were right angry with him, so that the doughty knight would have been killed by that blow. But Gawain started aside a little from the axe as it came gliding downwards to destroy him on that hillside, and shrank a little from that sharp iron with his shoulders. And the other withheld somewhat the shining weapon, and then reproved the princely knight with many a proud word. 'Thou art not Gawain,' said he, 'that is

holden to be so brave that never winced a hair by hill or valley, for now thou dost flee for fear, ere thou art hurt at all. Never heard I of such cowardice of that knight, neither did I shrink or flee when thou didst strike me, nor did I cavil at all in King Arthur's house. My head flew down to my foot, yet fled I not, and thou, ere any harm befell thee, waxest timid in heart. The better man of the two it behoves me to be called
        therefore.

    Quoth Gawain, 'I shrank once,
But so will I no more,
    Yet though my head fell on the stones
I cannot it restore.'

XIII

'BUT hasten thou, and let us come to the point. Deal me my destiny, and do it out of hand, for I will stand thee a stroke, and start aside no more till thine axe hath smitten me: have here my troth.' 'Have at thee then,' quoth that other, and he heaved the axe aloft and looked so angry that he might have been a madman. He struck at him mightily, but withheld his hand suddenly ere it could hurt him. Gawain promptly abided it and shrank in no limb of his body, but stood still as a stone or a tree stock that is rooted in the rocky ground with a hundred roots. Then merrily 'gan he speak, the man in green, 'So now thou hast thy heart whole and while it behoves me to smite. Hold high thy hood that Arthur gave thee, and keep thy neck to thy body lest it get in the way again.' Gawain then answered him full fiercely, and with heart sorrow,; Strike then, thou bold man; thou dost threaten too long. I hope that thy heart may wax timid.' 'Forsooth,' quoth that other, 'so fiercely thou dost speak, I will no longer hinder thee of

thine errand
right now.'
Then took he a stride to strike,
And wrinkled lips and brow,
No marvel it did him mislike,
Who hoped for no rescue now.

XIV

E raised lightly his axe and let it fall with the barb on his bare neck; and though he hotly hammered he did not hurt him much, but cut his skin a little. The sharp sword pierced through the flesh, so that the bright blood spurted over his shoulders to the ground; and when he saw the blood on the snow he started forward more than a spear length, hastily seized his helmet and put it on his head, and adjusted his shield; then brandishing forth a glittering sword, he spake fierce words, and never since his mother bare him was he half so merry. 'Cease now from thy strokes. Offer me no more. I have taken a blow in this place without striving; if thou givest me any more I will readily return

them, be ye of that well assured,
>　my foe.
>　　　But one stroke shall on me fall,
The covenant was right so
>　　　Made by us in Arthur's hall,
And therefore, knight, now ho!'

XV

THE man held back and rested upon his axe, set the shaft on the ground, and leaned on the point, looked at Sir Gawain, and saw how bravely he stood there, doughty and dreadless and fully armed, and in his heart he was well pleased. Then spake he merrily and loudly, with a rushing sound, and said, 'Bold man, on this hill be not thou so angry, for no man has done thee wrong, unmannerly nor in any wise, except as was agreed in the court of King Arthur. I promised thee a stroke thou hast it; hold thyself well payed. I hereby release thee of the remnant and of all other rights. Had I so liked, I could have dealt thee a worse blow; but first I menaced thee in playful wise, and cut thee not at all, though with right I proffered it to thee for the covenant made between us the first night when thou faithfully didst keep thy troth and gavest me all thy gain as a true man should. The second blow I gave thee for the morning when thou didst kiss my beautiful wife, and gavest me the kisses, and for the two kisses I gave thee here but

two blows without scathe
>   or tear.
A true man keeps his sooth,
And no scathe need he fear;
>   Thou didst flinch at the third, in truth,
So that stroke I gave thee here.

XVI

'OR in truth thou art wearing my weed in that same woven girdle which my wife gave to thee, as I wot well. And I know all about thy kisses and thy virtues also, and it was I myself who brought about the wooing of my wife. I sent her to assail thee, and I found thee to be the most faultless man on earth; as pearl is of more price than white pease, so is Gawain, in good faith, than all other gay knights. But, good sir, in this thou wast lacking a little in loyalty, not in any amorous working or wooing; but that thou didst love thy life the less I blame thee.' Then Sir Gawain stood thoughtful for a long time, and he trembled with rage, and all the blood of his body rushed to his face, and he shrank for shame all the time the Green Knight was talking. And

the first words he uttered were, 'A curse on both cowardice and covetousness! In them are both villany and vice, that destroy virtue.' Then he caught hold of the girdle and violently flung it at the knight. 'Lo, there is the false thing, and may evil befall it. For fear of thy stroke cowardice seized me, and for covetousness I was false to my nature, which is loyal and true as befitteth a knight. Now am I faulty and false and fearful. May sorrow betide Treachery and Untruth
      and Care.
I know thee knight here still.
All faulty is my fare,
      Let me but thwart thy will,
And after I will be ware.'

XVII

HEN the other laughed and said, 'I reck nought of the harm I had of thee, for thou hast made such clean confession of thy misdeeds, and hast done such penance at the point of my sword that I hold thee

free from thy fault and as innocent as if thou hadst never forfeited innocence since thou wast born. And here I give to thee again the girdle, that is gold hemmed and green as my gown. And thou shalt think on this chiding when thou goest forth among princes of price, and this shall be a pure token of thy chance at the Green Chapel, to chivalrous knights. Thou shalt come in this New Year and turn again to my dwelling, and we will spend the remnant of this noble feast in revellings as shall
     be seen.'

  Thus invited Sir Gawain the lord,
And quoth he 'My lady, I ween,
  She shall thee well accord,
Though she was thine enemy keen.'

XVIII

'NAY, forsooth,' quoth Gawain, and he seized his helmet, gracefully doffed it, and thanked the Green Knight. 'Sadly have I sojourned, and may joy betide thee from Him who hath all men in His keeping. Commend me to that courteous one thy

noble lady, and to the ancient dame, my honoured ladies who have so cunningly beguiled me. It is no wonder if a fool go mad in loving, and through the wiles of a woman be brought to sorrow, for so was Adam beguiled by one woman and Solomon by many; and to Samson, Delilah dealt him his weird, and David was beguiled by Barsabe, through whom he suffered great loss. All these were troubled by the wiles of women. Great joy it would be to love them well, and believe them not, if a man could do it. For of those who under heaven
>have mused,
All of them were beguiled
By women that they used;
>Though I be now be-wiled
I think I am excused.'

XIX

'BUT for thy girdle;' quoth Gawain, 'God reward thee for it, and I will wield it with good will, not for the gold, nor the samite, nor the silk, nor for its pendants, nor for weal nor worship, nor for its fair workings, but as a sign of my surfeit oft shall I look upon it; and when I ride in renown I shall

feel remorse for the fault and cowardice of the crabbed flesh, and how easy it is to be smirched by filth, and thus, when pride shall prick me through prowess of arms, the sight of this lovely lace shall moderate the beating of my heart. But one thing I pray thee, and may it not displease thee, since thou art lord of that land where I have sojourned with thee in worship and may the Lord reward thee that sitteth on high and upholds the heavens tell me thy name, and no more do I ask thee.' 'That shall I tell thee truly,' quoth that other. 'Bernlak de Haudesert I am called in this land; and through might of Morgan le Fay, who lodges in my house, and the cunning of the clergy, I am well learned in crafts. She was the mistress of Merlin, and many has she taken captive by her wiles. For she has made love for a long time to that famous clerk that knows all your knights
    at home.
  Morgan the goddess
Therefore is her name;
    There is no haughtiness
She cannot make full tame.'

XX

'IT was she who brought me in this wise to your joyous hall, to assay the pride thereof if it were truly spoken of, and to put to the test the great renown of the Round Table. She it was who made me do this marvel to put you all out of your wits, in order to vex and pain Guinevere and to cause her death, together with all that ghostly game and the knight with his head in his hand before the high table. It was the work of Morgan, who is that ancient dame thou didst see in my house. And she is thine aunt, and half-sister to Arthur, the daughter of the Duchess of Tintagel, who afterwards married Uther and gave birth to Arthur, who now is king. Therefore I implore thee, come and see thy aunt. Make merry in my house, for my servants all love thee, and I wish thee well, by my faith, as any man under heaven because of thy great truth.' But Sir Gawain denied with a nay, and said he would not in any wise. Then they embraced and kissed and commended each other to the King of Paradise, and they parted right there

        on the wold.

Gawain mounts horses, I ween,
To the king's town hastes him, bold.
The knight, in weeds of green,
Went o'er the moorland cold.

XXI

AWAIN rode over wild ways of the world. Sometimes he found rest in houses, and sometimes in the open air, and had many adventures in the valleys, and oft he overcame, and I will not try to tell it all.

The hurt was healed that he had in his neck, and he still carried the glittering belt at his side; under his left arm was the lace, tied with a knot, in token that he was taken in a fault. Thus he came to court, a knight all unhurt. There was joy in that hall when the great ones knew that Sir Gawain was come back, and great gain they thought it. The king kissed the knight, and the queen also, and many a faithful knight sought to embrace him, and they asked him of his faring, and he told them all the wonders thereof and all the labours he had endured, the chance of the chapel, the doings of the Green Knight, the love-making of the lady, and of the lace last of all. Then he showed them the cut in his neck which for his disloyalty he received at the hand of the Green Knight

>for blame.
>He moaned as he did it tell,
>The blood to his face then came,
>As he groaned for grief as well,
>When he showed it to them for shame.

XXII

'LO, my lord,' quoth the knight as he handled the lace, 'this is the bond and sign of my shame, this is the loss and the hurt that I have suffered through cowardice and covetousness. It is the token of untruth, and I must needs wear it while life shall last, for none may hide it, for when it is once fixed upon any one never will it pass from him.' The king comforted the knight, as did all the court; and they laughed loudly, and it was agreed that all the lords and ladies of the Round Table, each member of the brotherhood, should have a lace belt, a band of bright green, and wear it for the sake of Sir Gawain as long as they lived. And this was the renown of the Round Table, and he that had it was held in great honour for evermore, as I have seen it written in the best book of romance.

Thus in King Arthur's day did this adventure betide. The Brutus books bear witness to it, since the bold Knight Brutus came hither first after the siege and the assault ceased at Troy, as
>   I wis.
> Many adventures herebefore
> Have befallen such ere this.
>   Now He that thorn-crown for us bore
> Bring us to His bliss.   AMEN.

HONY SOYT QUI MAL PENCE

www.ingramcontent.com/pod-product-compliance
Lightning Source LLC
Chambersburg PA
CBHW072023110526
44592CB00012B/1413